DOWNSIDE OF DRUGS

Marijuana
Legal & Developmental Consequences

Rosa Waters

Mason Crest

Mason Crest
450 Parkway Drive, Suite D
Broomall, PA 19008
www.masoncrest.com

Printed and bound in the United States of America.

9 8 7 6 5 4 3 2

Series ISBN: 978-1-4222-3015-2
Hardcover ISBN: 978-1-4222-3022-0
Paperback ISBN: 978-1-4222-3192-0
ebook ISBN: 978-1-4222-8808-5

Cataloging-in-Publication Data on file with the Library of Congress.

Contents

DOWNSIDE
OF DRUGS

Marijuana

Legal & Developmental Consequences

DOWNSIDE OF DRUGS

ADHD Medication Abuse: Ritalin®, Adderall®, & Other Addictive Stimulants

Alcohol & Tobacco

Caffeine: Energy Drinks, Coffee, Soda, & Pills

Dangerous Depressants & Sedatives

Doping: Human Growth Hormone, Steroids, & Other Performance-Enhancing Drugs

Hard Drugs: Cocaine, LSD, PCP, & Heroin

Marijuana: Legal & Developmental Consequences

Methamphetamine & Other Amphetamines

New Drugs: Bath Salts, Spice, Salvia, & Designer Drugs

Over-the-Counter Medications

Prescription Painkillers: OxyContin®, Percocet®, Vicodin®, & Other Addictive Analgesics

INTRODUCTION

One of the best parts of getting older is the opportunity to make your own choices. As your parents give you more space and you spend more time with friends than family, you are called upon to make more decisions for yourself. Many important decisions that present themselves in the teen years may change your life. The people with whom you are friendly, how much effort you put into school and other activities, and what kinds of experiences you choose for yourself all affect the person you will become as you emerge from being a child into becoming a young adult.

One of the most important decisions you will make is whether or not you use substances like alcohol, marijuana, crystal meth, and cocaine. Even using prescription medicines incorrectly or relying on caffeine to get through your daily life can shape your life today and your future tomorrow. These decisions can impact all the other decisions you make. If you decide to say yes to drug abuse, the impact on your life is usually not a good one!

One suggestion I make to many of my patients is this: think about how you will respond to an offer to use drugs before it happens. In the heat of the moment, particularly if you're feeling some peer pressure, it can be hard to think clearly—so be prepared ahead of time. Thinking about why you don't want to use drugs and how you'll respond if you are asked to use them can make it easier to make a healthy decision when the time comes. Just like practicing a sport makes it easier to play in a big game, having thought about why drugs aren't a good fit for you and exactly what you might say to avoid them can give you the "practice" you need to do what's best for you. It can make a tough situation simpler once it arises.

In addition, talk about drugs with your parents or a trusted adult. This will both give you support and help you clarify your thinking. The decision is still yours to make, but adults can be a good resource. Take advantage of the information and help they can offer you.

Sometimes, young people fall into abusing drugs without really thinking about it ahead of time. It can sometimes be hard to recognize when you're making a decision that might hurt you. You might be with a friend or acquaintance in a situation that feels comfortable. There may be things in your life that are hard, and it could seem like using drugs might make them easier. It's also natural to be curious about new experiences. However, by not making a decision ahead of time, you may be actually making a decision without realizing it, one that will limit your choices in the future.

When someone offers you drugs, there is no flashing sign that says, "Hey, think about what you're doing!" Making a good decision may be harder because the "fun" part happens immediately while the downside—the damage to your brain and the rest of your body—may not be obvious right away. One of the biggest downsides of drugs is that they have long-term effects on your life. They could reduce your educational, career, and relationship opportunities. Drug use often leaves users with more problems than when they started.

Whenever you make a decision, it's important to know all the facts. When it comes to drugs, you'll need answers to questions like these: How do different drugs work? Is there any "safe" way to use drugs? How will drugs hurt my body and my brain? If I don't notice any bad effects right away, does that mean these drugs are safe? Are these drugs addictive? What are the legal consequences of using drugs? This book discusses these questions and helps give you the facts to make good decisions.

Reading this book is a great way to start, but if you still have questions, keep looking for the answers. There is a lot of information on the Internet, but not all of it is reliable. At the back of this book, you'll find a list of more books and good websites for finding out more about this drug. A good website is teens.drugabuse.gov, a site compiled for teens by the National Institute on Drug Abuse (NIDA). This is a reputable federal government agency that researches substance use and how to prevent it. This website does a good job looking at a lot of data and consolidating it into easy-to-understand messages.

What if you are worried you already have a problem with drugs? If that's the case, the best thing to do is talk to your doctor or another trusted adult to help figure out what to do next. They can help you find a place to get treatment.

Drugs have a downside—but as a young adult, you have the power to make decisions for yourself about what's best for you. Use your power wisely!

—Joshua Borus, MD

1. WHAT IS MARIJUANA?

Marijuana is a drug. That means it's a chemical that changes in some way the way your body works.

In many places around the world, it's against the law to use marijuana. Lots of people use marijuana, though. In fact, it's one of the most common illegal drugs. More than 300 million people around the world use marijuana. They like the way using marijuana makes them feel.

But marijuana has a downside!

When you think of the word "drug," you might think of pills. But not all drugs come in pill form. This is what marijuana usually looks like.

Chemicals are the building blocks that make up our world. Scientists think of them as tiny clusters of **molecules** that look like this model. Everything in the world is made of chemicals. But when a person brings the chemicals in a drug into her body, those chemicals change her body. The change can be good—like when an antibiotic kills an infection—or it can be bad—like when the chemicals in cigarettes cause cancer. Marijuana does not contain one single chemical—it has more than 400 different chemicals!

The most active chemical in marijuana is delta-9-tetrahydro-cannabinol, or THC. If you could see all the tiny pieces of a THC molecule, they would look like this. The more THC there is in marijuana, the stronger it is—and the more effect it will have on users. Today, marijuana contains more THC than it did thirty years ago. This means people feel a stronger "high"—but it also means that marijuana is more dangerous!

WHAT'S THE DOWNSIDE OF MARIJUANA?

Marijuana can mess up your life! It can make you sick. And it can make it hard for you to do well in school. Physical and mental side effects are only one side of the story, though. Using marijuana can get you in trouble with the law, and it can affect your *social life* as well.

Researchers have found that kids who regularly use marijuana often have less energy than other kids. They may have trouble concentrating. This can mean that they don't do as well on tests and homework. It's hard for them to pay attention in school.

Kids who are under the influence of marijuana may make stupid decisions. They may drive a car too fast or decide to have sex with someone they wouldn't have if they hadn't been stoned. Risky decisions like these can have serious consequences on the rest of their lives.

Regular marijuana use can get in the way of friendships. Marijuana users' poor judgment can make them do things that hurt others. Because they're not thinking clearly, marijuana users may not have very good communication skills. So marijuana can mess up your social life too!

Getting arrested for possessing or using marijuana goes on your record. It can limit your options for your college and career.

3. WHAT ARE THE LEGAL CONSEQUENCES OF USING MARIJUANA?

Using marijuana is illegal under U.S. *federal* law. However, some states have different laws in place. Many states have *decriminalized* marijuana. This means that if you're caught with marijuana and arrested, it's considered a *misdemeanor*. You'll probably have to pay a fine, the way you would if you got a traffic ticket, but you won't go to prison. However, in other states, possessing marijuana is still a more serious crime. Even in states that have decriminalized marijuana, if you're caught with large amounts of marijuana, you can face serious legal consequences. And if you're a repeat offender—in other words, if you've been caught more than once with marijuana—you can be arrested for a more serious crime.

Penalties for possessing marijuana may include:

- a fine (typically up to $2000)
- *mandatory* drug testing
- jail time
- drug awareness classes
- *probation*
- *electronic monitoring*

Driving under the influence of marijuana is against the law in many U.S. states. If you're caught, you can be arrested.

Growing marijuana or having drug paraphernalia (such as pipes and bongs) can also get you in greater legal trouble than just possessing marijuana.

If you're caught selling or giving marijuana to minors (people who are younger than 18), it's a more serious crime in many states. Being arrested for possession near a school, public park, or other community locations where kids might go can also have more serious consequences.

4. WHERE DOES MARIJUANA COME FROM?

Marijuana comes from a plant. It grows in many parts of the world. Its leaves are picked, and then dried. When people smoke or eat the leaves, they take the chemicals in the leaves into their bodies.

Because marijuana is a plant, sunshine, rainfall, and soil conditions will change how it grows. This means that marijuana that comes from one place might be stronger than marijuana that grows in another place. When you buy medicine at the drugstore, you know exactly what you're getting. When people use marijuana, they don't always know what they're getting. They can't be sure what to expect. They don't really know what they're doing to their heads!

Marijuana started out as a medicine. Today, many people think it should still be legal to use marijuana as a medicine. They say that just because marijuana can be *abused* doesn't mean that it couldn't still be used to help people. Many other legal medicines can be misused. Today, for example, many people abuse cold medicines and painkillers. These people use drugs to get high when those drugs were intended to help people who are sick or in pain.

The government makes sure that every drug that's labeled a certain way is exactly the same. But marijuana is illegal. No one controls how it's grown or packaged. It has no labels. Marijuana is produced and sold by criminals. Do you trust a guy like this to be careful about what he sells to people?

Human beings have been using the marijuana plant as a drug for thousands of years. This picture comes from a book that was written more than 1500 years ago. Back then, marijuana was used as a medicine. Long-ago doctors used it to treat earaches, sore joints, fever, and *insomnia*.

The marijuana plant has another use too. It has very tough *fibers*, which can be twisted into rope. Marijuana that is used for its fibers is usually called hemp. Marijuana first came to North America hundreds of years ago when the colonists brought hemp plants with them for making ropes.

17

5. HOW DO PEOPLE USE MARIJUANA?

Marijuana is usually smoked in hand-rolled cigarettes called joints. It can also be smoked in pipes, and in cigars, called blunts. Smoking is the most common way to use marijuana. Some people, though, brew the leaves into a tea. Sometimes people mix the dried leaves into baked goods.

A bong is a kind of marijuana pipe that has a place for water inside it, allowing the smoke to be filtered.

Different kinds of pipes are used for smoking marijuana.

Blunts are made by taking regular cigars and replacing the tobacco leaves inside with marijuana leaves. Blunts often contain other drugs as well as marijuana. Crack cocaine is one of the common ingredients. These other ingredients make blunts more dangerous.

The practice of mixing other drugs in with marijuana is called "lacing." People who use marijuana don't usually know if it has been laced. Marijuana can be laced with other drugs, but it can also be laced with substances that will just make it weigh more. Either way means users are taking in a lot more dangerous chemicals. Dealers do this in order to get more money for less marijuana. Sometimes marijuana is laced with powdered lead. Users who smoke lead have to go to the hospital!

6. HOW DOES MARIJUANA MAKE YOU FEEL?

People who use marijuana for **recreation** (and not as medicine), usually want to get "high." They are hoping the marijuana will make them feel happy and relaxed. What they will actually feel will depend on lots of things—like whether they've used marijuana before, how strong the marijuana is (how much THC it has), what they're expecting to feel, how they take the marijuana, and whether they're also drinking alcohol or using other drugs. Some people feel nothing at all when they smoke marijuana.

Sometimes marijuana does the opposite from what people are hoping. It can make people feel worried and scared. This is more likely to happen when the marijuana is stronger (has more THC in it).

Marijuana can change the way you see and feel. Things may look strange, and your hearing and your sense of touch may also send odd messages to your brain. Some of these *distorted* messages can be scary.

The effects of marijuana start as soon as 1 to 10 minutes after it is taken. It can last 3 to 4 hours or even longer.

Marijuana can make people feel thirsty and very hungry. People call this "the munchies." Marijuana users may become overweight as a result.

21

7. WHAT DOES MARIJUANA DO ONCE IT'S INSIDE YOUR BODY?

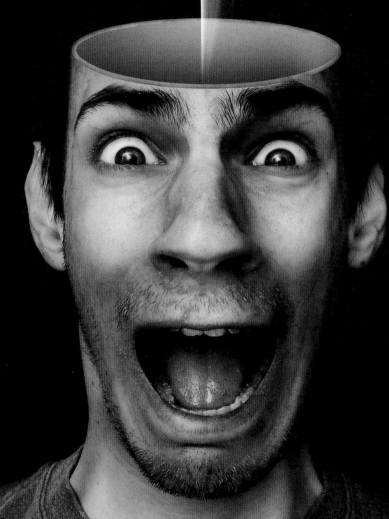

When marijuana smoke is **inhaled**, it doesn't actually go straight to your brain. Instead, it acts a little like to-bacco smoke—it passes through the lungs and into the bloodstream. From there it is carried to the organs (the heart, brain, lungs, stomach, liver, and so on). The fat in the body's organs **absorbs** the THC (the chemical in marijuana that makes people feel "high"). When a person smokes (or eats) marijuana it goes to all her organs.

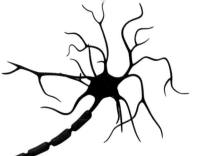

Once in the brain, the THC connects to nerve cells in different parts of the brain.

Your nerve cells pass messages between them throughout your body. They bring your body messages from your eyes or ears or skin, and they send messages back from your brain to your muscles and other parts of your body. Marijuana changes the way messages are passed between nerve cells.

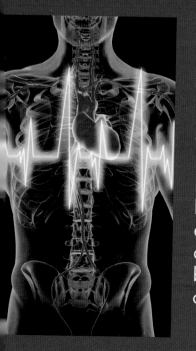

Marijuana changes the way other body organs work as well. For example, it makes the heart beat faster, as though a person had been running or exercising.

Marijuana mixes up the pieces of your brain that usually work together. It especially changes the parts of the brain that control memory, *concentration* and thought, pleasure, sense of time, the senses, and movement. This is why marijuana changes the way a person feels, thinks, and moves.

23

8. HOW DOES MARIJUANA CHANGE YOUR BRAIN?

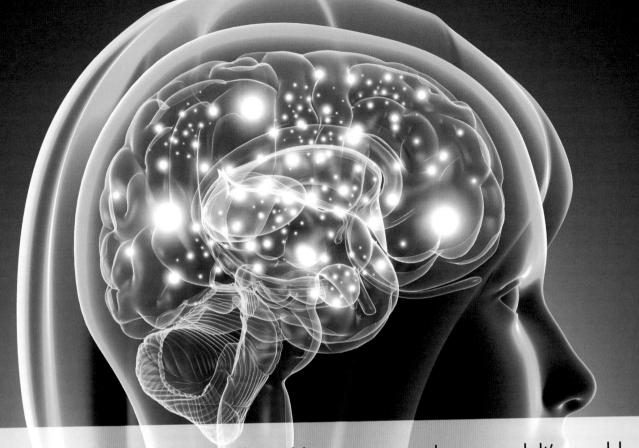

Your brain will be more affected by marijuana than an adult's would be. That's because a young person's brain is different from an adult brain in many ways. Teenagers are likely to feel things more intensely than adults do. They often make decisions based on their emotions rather than reason. That's because the limbic system, the area of the brain that controls memory and emotions, is highly developed in a teenager, while the prefrontal cortex, the area responsible for judgment, is still developing.

Certain brain centers, such as the limbic system, are more influenced by THC (tetrahydrocannabinol), the active ingredient in marijuana. This means the same centers responsible for memory formation, emotion, aggression, and fear are also the ones most affected by marijuana. So marijuana affects adolescents more than it does adults.

3 X

Marijuana use is three times more likely to lead to **dependence** among adolescents than among adults. The earlier kids start using marijuana, the more likely they are to become dependent on this or other illicit drugs later in life.

Researchers have found that people who begin using marijuana when they're young damage their brains' ability to reason and learn. Their intelligence levels decrease. In other words, marijuana can make you stupid!

The chemicals in marijuana change the way brain cells communicate with each other. This makes users feel laid back and "mellow." But in young adults, this laid-back, lazy feeling can become permanent. When this happens, they may not have the **ambition** they need to succeed and **excel** in life. Most people don't get paid or win awards for sitting around watching TV!

9. HOW CAN MARIJUANA MAKE YOU SICK?

Smoking marijuana daily can hurt your immune system. You have cells in your bronchial passages that protect your body against any germs you breathe in—but smoking kills these cells. This means that germs are more likely to get inside your body. Marijuana also damages your body's ability to fight off germs once they get inside. You're more likely to get seriously sick or even die if you get something that you would otherwise have recovered from.

Marijuana use may cause people who have HIV to develop AIDS.

Scientists have found that marijuana contains a chemical that triggers the body to produce a certain kind of cell. This cell keeps the immune system from doing its job. People with a lot of these cells not only catch colds and the flu more often, they also are more likely to have serious cancers. Cancer happens when abnormal cells grow somewhere inside your body. The unhealthy cancer cells push out the normal, healthy cells. Marijuana can make cancer cells grow faster.

10. WHAT DOES MARIJUANA DO TO YOUR LUNGS?

When most people think of lung cancer, they think of cigarette smoke. However, marijuana can cause the same results, since both kinds of smoke contain many of the same *toxic* chemicals. Marijuana may even be more of a cancer threat than tobacco, since it contains four times the amount of tar that one regular cigarette does. Marijuana smoke also contains 50 to 75 percent more of the hydrocarbons that are proven to be *carcinogenic*. When you add this to the fact that people smoking a joint are more likely to hold the smoke in longer and breathe it in deeper than tobacco users do, marijuana users could be putting themselves at an even greater risk of developing cancer than tobacco users are.

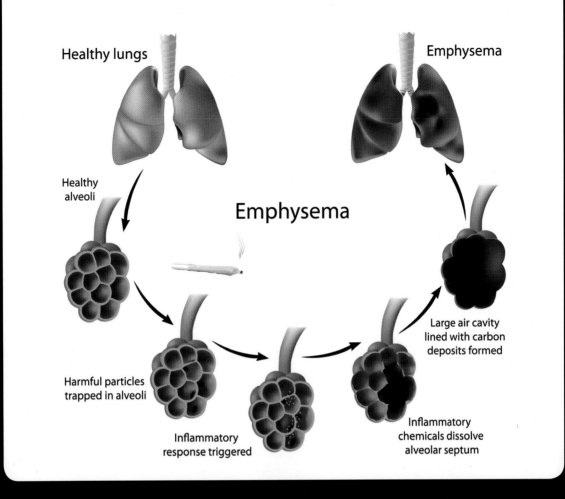

Healthy lungs

Emphysema

Emphysema

Healthy
alveoli

Harmful particles
trapped in alveoli

Inflammatory
response triggered

Inflammatory
chemicals dissolve
alveolar septum

Large air cavity
lined with carbon
deposits formed

Lung cancer is not the only bad thing weed can do to your lungs. Marijuana smoke can also cause diseases like **emphysema**, **chronic bronchitis**, and **respiratory** infections. The **toxins** in the marijuana cause the air passages in the lungs to become narrower. This means they don't work as well, and the lungs easily become **inflamed**.

Researchers have found that people who smoke marijuana regularly get more colds than people who don't. They also miss more work, because they're sick more often.

29

11. WHAT DOES MARIJUANA DO TO YOUR HEART?

Studies have shown that the chance of a heart attack goes up by more than four times in the first hour after someone smokes marijuana. While scientists are not sure why this occurs, they think it may be because marijuana use increases blood pressure and heart rate. It also causes the blood to lose some of its ability to carry oxygen, making the heart work harder. All these factors lead to the ideal conditions for a heart attack.

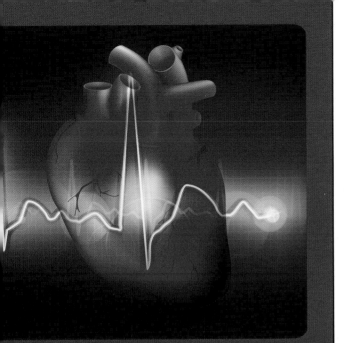

Doctors recommend that people should not smoke marijuana who have heart disease or are at risk of having a heart attack.

Marijuana can cause heart palpitations. This means that you feel like your heart is pounding or racing. Marijuana can also cause heart arrhythmias, which means that instead of beating at a steady rhythm, your heart rate may speed up and then slow down suddenly.

Smoking weed can make your heart beat as much as 100 percent faster. This happens immediately, as soon as you smoke marijuana, but it can last for up to three hours.

12. CAN MARIJUANA CAUSE MENTAL ILLNESS?

Researchers have found a connection between marijuana and mental disorders like *panic attacks*, *flashbacks*, *delusions*, *paranoia*, and *hallucinations*. Marijuana has also been known to cause flare-ups in people who already have mental illnesses such as *bipolar disorder* and *schizophrenia*.

Even smoking weed once can affect your mental state. Between 10 and 15 percent of people who smoked marijuana for the first time said that they felt confused or paranoid after using the drug. This is caused by the THC attaching itself to brain cells.

Teenagers who use marijuana weekly have double the risk of depression later in life.

Young people ages twelve through seventeen who smoke marijuana weekly are three times more likely than nonusers to have suicidal thoughts.

Some research indicates that teenagers who use marijuana frequently have a greater chance of having schizophrenia later

13. WHAT DOES MARIJUANA DO TO THE REPRODUCTIVE SYSTEM?

Marijuana use affects the reproductive systems of both men and women. Smoking a lot of weed changes your sex organs. If you're a male, marijuana will lower your testosterone levels. Testosterone is the *hormone* that makes men have deeper voices, grow beards, and develop muscles—so if you have less testosterone, you look less like a man and more like a woman. If you're a female who uses marijuana regularly, you may get more pimples. You may start to get more body hair,

Men who smoke a lot of weed may not be able to have an erection. They many not produce sperm.

Girls who use marijuana regularly may stop getting their periods.

Heavy marijuana use can permanently damage a woman's eggs. This could mean that she will never be able to get pregnant, even if later in life, she stops using marijuana.

Using marijuana during pregnancy can lead to mis-carriages. Babies who are born to mothers who are marijuana users are often born prematurely or with low birth weights.

 14. HOW DOES MARIJUANA CHANGE HOW WELL YOU DO IN SCHOOL?

Young adults who use marijuana are less likely to graduate. They get lower grades in class and on *standardized* tests. While two people may score equally well on tests in fourth grade, by the time both are seniors in high school, if one of the people is a marijuana smoker, he will score significantly lower on tests than the other student who doesn't smoke weed.

Marijuana can hinder your ability to learn. Smoking weed can make it hard to concentrate and remember what you've learned.

Marijuana use is linked to poorer grades. A young person with a "D" average is four times more likely to have used marijuana than a student with an "A" average.

Marijuana use is linked to higher dropout rates. Students who use marijuana are more than twice as likely to quit school before they graduate than non-users.

15. WHAT ABOUT MARIJUANA AND DRIVING?

When you're stoned, you are less coordinated. You can't concentrate as well, and your reaction time is slower. This can make driving very dangerous. If you're driving under the influence of marijuana and an animal or child runs onto the road, you may not be able to stop in time. You might get in an accident with another car or go off the road. You could hurt or kill someone. You yourself could end up in the hospital or dead.

After four or six hours have gone by since someone has smoked marijuana, she won't feel high anymore. But her coordination, concentration, and reaction time will still be reduced, even thought she doesn't know it. She may think she's okay to drive—but she's not.

Reaction time for motor skills, such as driving, is reduced by 41 percent after smoking one joint and is reduced 63 percent after smoking two joints.

When reckless drivers were tested at the scene for drugs, more than 33 percent tested positive for marijuana.

Driving under the influence of marijuana is against the law, even in states where the recreational or medicinal use of marijuana is legal.

16. MORE QUESTIONS?

Doesn't marijuana just make people mellow?

Not always. Marijuana use has been connected with violent behavior. Young adults who use marijuana weekly are four times more likely to engage in violent behavior than those who don't.

If I use marijuana, how does that hurt anyone?

Marijuana *trafficking* is a big, often violent business, at home and abroad. It can lead to other crimes, including murder. When you buy marijuana, you're supporting that business.

Can smoking marijuana harm or even kill me?

Marijuana is not usually toxic enough to kill you, but if you mix this drug with other drugs or do something that requires brain skills and coordination (like driving a car), then yes, smoking weed can kill you.

How does smoking marijuana increase the dangers from getting drunk?

Smoking marijuana suppresses your body's *instinctual* need to throw-up bad things in your stomach. If you have been smoking pot while binge drinking, your body will not be able to *purge* when your blood alcohol level reaches a dangerous level.

If I get caught using marijuana, can that hurt my chances of getting into college?

Getting into a good college is harder than ever these days. Most colleges and universities will check all your high school student records. A history of drug use, possession, buying, or selling drugs may kill your chances of getting into the college or university of your choice.

FURTHER READING

Berlatsky, Noah. *Marijuana (Opposing Viewpoints)*. Farmington Hills, Mich.: Greenhaven, 2012.

Brown, Wain. *Facts About Marijuana*. Tallahassee, Fla.: William Gladden Foundation, 2011.

DeRamus, Tony. *The Secret Addiction: Overcoming Marijuana Dependency*. New York: SMA, 2011.

Earleywine, Mitch. *Understanding Marijuana*. New York: Oxford, 2005.

Lawton, Sandra Augustyn (ed.). *Drug Information for Teens: Health Tips About the Physical and Mental Effects of Substance Abuse: Including Information About Marijuana, Inhalants, Club Drugs, Stimulants, Hallucinogens, Opiates, Prescription and Over-the-Counter Drugs, Herbal Products, Tobacco, Alcohol, and More*. Detroit, Mich.: Omnigraphics, 2006.

McMullan, Jordan. *Marijuana*. Farmington Hills, Mich.: Thomson Gale, 2004.

Mehling, Randi. *Marijuana*. New York: Chelsea House, 2003.

National Institute on Drug Abuse. *Heads Up: Real News About Drugs and Your Body*. New York: Scholastic, 2003.

National Institute of Health. *Marijuana: Facts for Teens*. Washington, D.C.: Penny Hill, 2012.

Roffman, Roger, Alan Budney, Denise Walker, and Robert Stephens. *Marijuana Dependence and Its Treatment*. Sheffield, UK: All About Psychology, 2011.

Somdahl, Gary L. *Marijuana Drug Dangers*. Berkeley Heights, N.J.: Enslow, 2002.

FIND OUT MORE ON THE INTERNET

Brain Power! The NIDA Junior Scientist Program
www.drugabuse.gov/JSP/JSP.html

NIDA Infofacts: Understanding Drug Abuse and Addiction
www.drugabuse.gov/Infofax/understand.html

NIDA Sites on Marijuana:
www.nida.nih.gov/MarijBroch/MarijIntro.html
www.nida.nih.gov/Infofax/marijuana.html
www.nida.nih.gov/ResearchReports/marijuana
www.drugabuse.gov/drugpages/marijuana.html
www.marijuana-info.org

GLOSSARY

absorbs: Takes in or soaks up.

abused: Used a drug in a way that hurts you.

ambition: Wanting to achieve something.

bipolar disorder: A psychiatric disorder in which a persons emotions can swing from extreme depression to extreme excitement.

bronchitis: When the tubes in your lungs become inflamed. It can cause severe coughing.

carcinogenic: Something that causes cancer.

chronic: A health condition that lasts a long time.

concentration: Paying attention to something for a long time.

decriminalized: Made something no longer a crime.

delusions: Having beliefs that are obviously false.

dependence: Relying on something; needing something in order to function.

distorted: Twisted out of shape so that it looks strange or scary.

electronic monitoring: When the government uses electronic devices to keep track of where you are and what you're doing.

emphysema: A health condition where the lungs become less elastic and can't hold as much air.

excel: To do very well at something.

federal: On a national level.

flashbacks: Sudden scary memories from your past.

fibers: Tiny threads or strands. They can be used to make rope or fabric.

hallucinations: Seeing or hearing things that aren't there.

hormone: A chemical produced by your body. Hormones do things like regulate how fast you digest food, make your body grow, and develop certain body characteristics.

inflamed: When a part of your body becomes red, swollen, and irritated.

inhaled: Breathed in.

insomnia: A condition where you're unable to fall asleep normally.

instinctual: Having to do with a skill or behavior that you have naturally.

mandatory: Required by law.

misdemeanor: A minor crime.

molecules: The smallest parts of a chemical. A molecule is made up of atoms arranged in a certain way.

panic attacks: Feelings of intense fear and anxiety that sometimes feel like having a heart attack.

paranoia: Suspicion and fear that people or the world are out to get you.

probation: When the government keeps track of you to make sure you won't commit another crime.

purge: To expel something harmful from your body.

recreation: Something done just for fun.

respiratory: Having to do with your lungs or with breathing.

schizophrenia: A severe mental illness where someone's connection to reality breaks down.

social life: The time you spend with friends and other people.

standardized: Tests that are designed to be the same for a very wide range of people.

toxic: Poisonous.

toxins: Poisonous substances.

trafficking: The business of trading and selling an illegal product.

INDEX

PICTURE CREDITS

ABOUT THE AUTHOR
AND THE CONSULTANT

ROSA WATERS lives in New York State. She has worked as a writer for several years, producing works on health, history, and other topics.

DR. JOSHUA BORUS, MD, MPH, graduated from the Harvard Medical School and the Harvard School of Public Health. He completed a residency in pediatrics and then served as chief resident at Floating Hospital for Children at Tufts Medical Center before completing a fellowship in Adolescent Medicine at Boston Children's Hospital. He is currently an attending physician in the Division of Adolescent and Young Adult Medicine at Boston Children's Hospital and an instructor of pediatrics at Harvard Medical School.